Credit Repair

How to Build Great Credit and Raise Your Credit Score.

© Copyright 2017 Connection Books Club- All Rights Reserved.

This document is presented with the desire to provide reliable, quality information about the topic in question and the facts discussed within. This Book is sold under the assumption that neither the publisher or the author should be asked to provide the services discussed within. If any discussion, professional or legal, is otherwise required a proper professional should be consulted.

The reproduction, duplication or transmission of any of the included information is considered illegal whether done in print or electronically. Creating a recorded copy or a secondary copy of this work is also prohibited unless the action of doing so is first cleared through the Publisher and condoned in writing. All rights reserved.

Any information contained in the following pages is considered accurate and truthful and that any liability through inattention or by any use or misuse of the topics discussed within falls solely on the reader. There are no cases in which the Publisher of this work can be held responsible or be asked to provide reparations for any loss of monetary gain or other damages which may be caused by following the presented information in any way shape or form.

The following information is presented purely for informative purposes and is therefore considered universal. The information presented within is done so without a contract or any other type of assurance as to its quality or validity.

Any trademarks which are used are done so without consent and any use of the same does not imply consent or permission was gained from the owner. Any trademarks or brands found within are purely used for clarification purposes and no owners are in anyway affiliated with this work.

Table of Contents

Introduction 1
Credit, Credit Scores, And Fico.. 5
Removing Credit Score Hindrances....................................... 10
Credit Disputes.. 14
Improve Credit History 18
Automatic Payments Equal Consistency............................. 22
Secured Credit Card 25
Attach To A Family Account 29
Get An Increased Limit.. 35
Multiple Monthly Payments.. 38
Keep Old Credit Accounts Open 41
Have Multiple Credit Types 44
Pay Debt As You Go.. 47
Credit Utilization Ratio.. 50
Keep "Credit" Below 30% Income 52
Seek Credit Unions 55
Paying Off Installment Accounts.. 58
Chapter 17: Pay Off Debt... 60
Lower Interest Rate Last 62
Lower Balance First 65
Student Loans And Scores.. 68
Wrap Up: Credit Repair Overview.. 74

Introduction

September 11, 2001, is a day that changed many people's lives, whether you were directly affected by a loss of a loved one or your financial world changed because you depended on travel for work. This day in history can be described in a variety of ways. One way is that people were given the impression that flying on an airplane was not as safe as advertised. Two, tighter airport regulations were necessary. Three, when the masses are scared, their way of life will change, if only for a short time. Several small companies and independent contractors suffered job or financial losses. Many saw the inside of a bankruptcy courtroom because of the change in everyone's mind that perhaps traveling is not safe.

One couple would drive snowbird's vehicles from New England to Florida each year, but in that year, those people stayed home. The couple also helped move cars for people moving, who couldn't drive their cars to their new destination. This stopped as well. The bills didn't also stop, so missed payments rose.

It was during this time that an explosion of changes started in the bankruptcy world due to the sheer number of people needing to file. It would take until 2004 for some of the changes to take effect, but already a need for information was forming, such as information about credit scores and repairing debt that largely seemed a mystery.

Starting around 2003 and to this day, there have been several books on credit repair, secret strategies for building great credit and raising fallen credit scores. These strategies have always existed, but perhaps no one truly had to go looking for them in the same "mass" searching that went on since the financial after effects of 2001. The 2007-2008 financial crisis has only intensified the need for this knowledge.

You can equate the 20 subjects covered in this book as having been around for decades, but popularized since the new millennium. The internet is partially to thank for the accessibility of the information. Add in the financial implosions that have occurred to more than half of the American population, and it makes sense that starting about 2003 these strategies became known.

Contributors to the strategies in this book include names like Steven Snyder, writers for Myfico.com, Credit Karma, Credit.com, Huffington Post, Nerd Wallet's Sean McMurray, and just about any freelance writer out there. The difference between the contributor information you find as you do the research and this book is accessibility.

You don't have to waste five hours looking up each resource named in this book. You don't have to spend another five hours examining testimonials or wondering if you can believe what is written on a website. Instead, you have an outline of the strategy, how it works, personal and public information that will make these strategies worth believing in. There is no hype, no selling you some "secret" strategy, or trying to snowball you into giving out personal data. You don't have to wonder if another identity thief is going to ruin your credit or if your bankruptcy/financial troubles will follow you until you die.

You have the answers here. So, if you believe in fairies, Santa Claus, leprechauns, elves, and gnomes—this book is not for you. It is for people who trust in good ol' fashioned common sense and the knowledge of how the credit scoring system works.

Thank you for your purchase of this eBook! I hope you enjoy reading this eBook as much as I enjoyed writing it. As part of your purchase, I invite you to join my email subscribers. This FREE subscription lets you receive a newsletter, highlighting the great new books available from Connection Books Club and other exclusive business and self development information. Subscribing is easy, and members receive great deals and fantastic eBooks at a discount! All you need to do is click this link to enter your email:

http://www.connectionbooksclub.com/bonus/

In addition to this great opportunity to subscribe to incredible discounts and our newsletter, as a welcome gift, you'll receive a FREE eBook download! Learn how to secure your financial future with the informative eBook, *Money Management: Learn How to Organize Your Financial Life and Invest in Your Future*. It's yours for FREE once you've enrolled!

http://www.connectionbooksclub.com/bonus/

Welcome to the club, and we hope you enjoy your purchase as well as our FREE welcome gift!

Have you ever wished that you were better with money?

Do you ever find yourself being overwhelmed by the state of your personal finances?

Would you like to become more financially responsible?

Now you can, with **5 Reasons to Invest in Money Management: Learn How to Organize Your Financial**

Life and Invest in Your Future, a short self-help book that is packed with information on how to make the most of your financial situation.

If you want to be able to lower your interest rates, learn up to date money management strategies and turn your financial situation into one of prosperity and stability, then you'll find the answers inside, with solid advice that includes:

- Strategies which are designed for the average person
- Your options for retirement
- Hacks for navigating the grocery store's subtle spending traps
- Ways to pay less than you owe on credit cards and other outstanding debts
- Finding freedom with financial stability

Suitable for complete novices, **5 Reasons to Invest in Money Management** is a book that will transform the way you look at and deal with your finances.

Download a free copy and start investing in your future today! http://www.connectionbooksclub.com/bonus/

Prosperity is waiting for **YOU!**

Credit, Credit Scores, and FICO

What do Credit, Credit Scores, and FICO mean to your Credit Report

When it comes to your credit report, there are three types of credit accounts: revolving, installment, and open. You might have thought the discussion would be about secured or unsecured, but in actuality, credit reporting agencies look at credit differently. Speaking of credit reporting agencies—there are three of them. You will want to get to know these three companies intimately: Equifax, Transunion, and Experian.

Revolving Credit

Revolving credit requires you to make a different payment amount each month based on how much of the credit line you utilize. This sound an awful lot like credit card usage because that is one of the most used types of revolving credit people have. The statistic is that the average household in the USA has at least three credit cards in their wallet. Nerd Wallet did a study that indicates $15,310 of household debt is on credit cards. If you say the average family is two adults and one child, then there are at least three credit cards each in the parent's wallets and one credit card for the child as well. The accounts can be tied, meaning the parents have opened three credit card accounts with joint access and named their children on one of those accounts.

There are other types of revolving credit. HELOCs or home equity lines of credit are revolving credit accounts because you can withdraw as you need the funds and what you owe is based on how much you withdraw from the line of credit.

Revolving credit is also defined by the monthly payment and interest. Monthly payments with revolving credit require a minimum amount, where the majority of the balance can be paid off later. As long as there is an unpaid balance for the line of credit, there is also interest to be collected by the creditor.

Installment Credit

Installment credit requires a fixed payment each month based on the fixed period one has to pay it off. There is also interest attached to the credit, which is also based on the period you have to repay the debt. Installment agreements can either be secured or unsecured loans, such as mortgages, student loans, auto loans, business loans, and home equity loans.

Installment credit is acceptable credit. It is not a bad type of credit to have because it helps you build your credit history. However, not all installment credit is treated equally. For example, student loans are weighted differently than mortgages. This will matter when discussing certain strategies for building great credit.

Open Credit

Open credit is an account that you must pay off each month, in full. There is no interest and no reduced monthly payment due to an installment agreement. Typically, if you do not pay off this debt each month, then there is a late fee charged by the company. Open credit accounts are mobile phone accounts, charge cards/store cards, and home utilities. Open credit is rarely reported to the credit reporting agencies.

Often, a report is made, when a person is delinquent in the payment. Occasionally, this type of creditor will make a report every three months. It just depends on the company. In the last 5 years, many utility companies and cell phone companies have started running a person's credit, weighing their credit history and scores, and determined fees and plans. It is due to delinquency. A high number of delinquent accounts exist because a person moves, ignores their utility payments, and the company has trouble tracking them down.

You might have noticed a change, when you switched your internet service provider or cable TV provider. These companies have started asking for social security numbers in order to run your credit history. It means a tighter industry, where people can no longer be delinquent, and the potential for more accounts to appear in your credit history. The changes only matter, if you have consistently been delinquent on these accounts. If you pay on time every month, you don't have to worry about the company sending a report.

Credit Scores and FICO

Experian, Equifax, and Transunion all provide you with credit scores, but you have to understand that not all credit scores are the FICO score. FICO scores are created by the Fair Isaac Corporation. No one knows for certain how the Fair Isaac Corporation creates their score because it is a proprietary formula. It has been released that the score is based on five categories, which are weighted differently with regard to importance. These categories are:

- Payment History
- Amount Owed
- Length of History
- New Credit
- Type of Credit

To break it down, each contributes with a percentage towards the score, where the payment history is 35%, and type of credit used is 10%. The other percentages are 30%, 15%, and 10%, respective of the order listed in the bullet points. The FICO score places a lot of emphasis on the payment history and amount owed. Payment history assesses things like being on time, late, delinquent, or going through a bankruptcy as more important than the types of credit and new credit you might have.

One of the biggest questions that has come up in recent years, particularly since 2008, is the discrepancy of credit scores. For example, Transunion started offering credit scores via certain credit cards like Discover. Yet, when a person went to buy a car loan, the score on their Discover card account was different than the FICO score used for the loan.

There is a consumer version of your credit score that can be released by the three credit reporting agencies. They use a slightly different formula, as do some of the credit card companies. Unless you have a piece of paper that states the score is from FICO, such as those handed to you by lenders when you go to get a loan, you may be seeing your consumer credit score versus your FICO score.

Before you start using various strategies to repair your credit score and build better credit overall, you have to be willing to pay for your credit score either through Myfico.com or one of the three credit reporting agencies. If you see a score for free, it is generally the consumer score versus the one using the proprietary calculation FICO uses. The difference between them will matter.

The FICO score is between 300 and 850, with higher scores indicating lower credit risk. If you walk into a bank asking for a mortgage thinking you have a score close to 800, only to find out your FICO score is 750, you are going to want to know why, and what you can do to get the other 50 back. The thing is you haven't lost it, in the sense that something is harming your credit, but that FICO never provided it to you.

Now that you have a clear understanding of what credit is, the consumer credit scores, and FICO, you are ready to discover some strategies that can be of use to build great credit and raise your credit scores.

Removing Credit Score Hindrances

Nothing Brings your Credit Down Faster than Missed Payments

Up until about 2004, no one thought that you could remove items from your credit history. But, about the time many were seeking debt solutions, there were equally just as many seeking a way to repair their earlier credit score drops. Overnight, companies offered both legitimate and scam debt solutions for credit repair. It was also a time for the revelation of certain tightly kept "secrets." Perhaps it is that no one bothered to try to remove missed payments and other items from their credit history. Maybe no one paid enough attention to their credit reports, until identity theft started to rear its ugly head through numerous online scams. What matters to you—is that savvy people like Stephen Snyder started getting their credit reports sent to them and started reading the fine print.

In the fine print and through asking questions to the credit bureau representatives, many found that you could remove items from your credit report.

Credit score hindrances or credit score killers as Credit.com coins them, are missed payments and late payments that have happened once or sporadically. For example, one young college student, newly graduated, moved twice after graduating. The only address for this person was her parents' old home. Her parents didn't live there anymore because they had moved away two years prior.

The student loan company was ready to take the student out of deferred status for being a full-time student. Her loan was coming due. By the time the company found her new address, she was late, and her credit report cited an inability to contact her. The student loan company, through a Federal program, reports every month if there is an on time payment, late payment, or missed payment. Pretty much as soon as the young woman started building credit, she had a missed payment.

Your missed or late payments can arise for any number of reasons. It is not how this student obtained the status of one month missed payment, but what she learned could be done about it. This knowledge came from various online sources, as well as Stephen Snyder as part of a bankruptcy credit repair concept. However, it works for anyone who has something they missed just once.

Removing the Hindrance to a Higher Score

This strategy is all about timing. You cannot just remove a late or missed payment from your credit score because it reflects badly on your score. It is a part of your history and it matters when calculating your score. However, there is a general rule that all credit reporting bureaus follow and it is this "secret" that was revealed during the last decade.

- Any late or missed payment can be removed if it is older than seven years.

If the year is 2017, then anything prior to 2010 can be removed from your credit report. It does not matter what type of account it was or the reason behind the late or missed payment. As long as you have not gone through a bankruptcy with that credit account, it can be removed after it is seven years old.

Most credit reporting agencies should automatically remove the credit accounts from seven years ago; especially, if they are closed. However, it does not mean they will. To assume something will "automatically" fall off after seven years is a mistake, because it may not happen and it can continue to hurt your credit score.

You have three ways to utilize this strategy of removing hindrances to a higher score:

1. Contact the creditor. Speak directly to the creditor or send a "goodwill" letter asking for an adjustment of your credit report. The creditor may not be willing to send an amended report to the credit bureaus.

2. Contact each credit bureau and ask for the removal of the older information. However, be aware if it is only one month and you have had the account for 20 years, the length of time you have had the account matters to the overall calculation. One month with a missed or late payment will not reflect as badly as if you have entire history with that credit account of making late payments. Your credit report will reflect when you opened the account, so you certainly don't need a running history in arrears if it is old enough to be removed.

3. Try negotiating with the creditor if they are not willing to have the information removed, or if the credit bureaus are not working fast enough. By negotiating for automatic payments, you may be able to get the 8th year and older reporting information removed. Not all companies will work this way.

It takes time for items to fall off. You cannot expect to pull up a report in a month and have the item removed. Sometimes creditors only report every three months, thus if you have just hit the reporting time, you have to wait for the next cycle to occur for new information to appear.

You can always dispute a claim on your credit report by contacting the bureaus; however, if you dispute too many late or missed payments when your history is full of them—you won't see results.

This strategy of removing hindrances to increase your credit score is about taking the odd man out of the equation. It works only for items that are 7 years old.

Also understand that not all credit bureaus move as quickly as others. Transunion has been known to be extremely slow in removing old debts or debts not associated with you. It is often about what is actually affecting your report versus what you feel should or should not be on there. If the record is not harming your report enough, the company may be unwilling to act quickly. It can take several letters before you see a change.

Key Points

- This works for a once or twice late or missed payment issue.
- It is for debts that are seven years or older.
- Contact the creditor first.
- Try the credit bureau if the creditor will not help.
- Make a deal to set up automatic payments if the first two options don't work.
- Give it at least four months before you look at your credit report again.

Credit Disputes

Dispute all Inaccuracies; They Steal from your Score

Is there something on your credit report that is not correct? Perhaps it is an address you never lived at? Maybe, it is a credit account you never opened? The fact is – even the credit bureaus are not perfect. A single error can occur based on your name's spelling or an incorrect number in your social security number. If something has been associated with your personal information, then you could find your credit report filled with inaccurate data.

There is an individual who, when she looks up her name, is associated with a 60+ individual and she is only in her 30s. It has to do with her name and a previous address being in the same town. It is not fair for the association to be made, but it has been, so now the person has to make certain all recorded information on her credit reports is only associated with places she has lived, companies she has allowed to run her credit, and the credit accounts she has opened.

Credit disputes are not a new issue. Since the time the credit bureaus were formed to assess credit history and provide a score, credit disputes have occurred. The current credit reporting agencies have evolved from the 1950s. At the time, three companies in the Tristate (Delaware, New Jersey, and Pennsylvania) area were just called the Bureaus. Their function was the same—to track consumer behavior, focusing primarily on bank, retailer, and finance company information. Now more credit disputes are occurring because of the sheer number of products available and the electronic system through which creditors report.

You can think of this as a second step to removing hindrances from your credit reports. Hindrances can also be under the guise of disputes, as long as you are not lying about the information you want removed. It is also very rare for any inaccuracy to actually help your credit score. The only way it can help is if the account is in good standing and it is an older item that is considered a "better" credit account to have.

How it Works

Anytime you receive a physical copy of your credit report from any agency and it has an inaccurate detail, you can fill out the dispute section that came with the paperwork. You will need to use the entire space available, and if necessary, write an addendum to explain your request and proof of the inaccuracy.

The credit bureau(s) will assess the details, determine the validity, and remove the incorrect item as long as there is sufficient evidence.

It can take up to three months for the removal to occur. For some things, such as an incorrect address associated with your account or a phone number, it can take even longer.

The credit bureaus are worried about miss-assigned debt versus the accuracy of your telephone numbers or addresses. One person had to write five times before an incorrect address was removed from his credit report.

A Quicker Alternative

If you have already accessed your credit report via an online portal such as Credit Karma, Credit Report, or directly through the bureaus, then you can file an online dispute.

The dispute works the same way. You provide all inaccurate data, the proof of why it is wrong, and ask for it to be removed.

For some this is easier because you don't have to worry about mailing in the documents, you can just submit the dispute in a few minutes after looking over your credit report.

Incorrect information will bring down your credit score when it affects your credit history and amount owed. Addresses and phone numbers are less likely to affect your score, unless through these inaccuracies credit accounts become associated with your history and accounts.

You also don't want to leave anything incorrect on your score in the unlikely event that someone can glean information from it. Identity thieves can use an address or phone number to affect your credit, all it takes is one incorrect usage of an address and access to your credit report to trick a company into making a huge sale in your name.

Key Points

- There are two methods to dispute an incorrect item.
- Incorrect items can negatively affect your score.
- Inaccuracies need to be removed.

Enjoying your eBook so far? Take a moment to subscribe to our FREE newsletter for incredible discounts, books giveaways, and VIP offers!

➢ http://www.connectionbooksclub.com/bonus/

All we need is your email, and you'll be set up to receive more of the eBooks you can't wait to read.

Improve Credit History

Beginning Paying your Debts on Time by Establishing a Budget

It seems so simple, and it is. Every credit repair strategy you are going to see online or in books will tell you the same thing—you can repair your credit by paying on time. The first steps to improving your credit history are getting credit score hindrances and inaccuracies off your report. They ding your score and are unnecessary score killers. Of course, if you have missed a late payment that is not more than seven years old, it will have to remain on your report. This rule of seven years is where improving your credit history in the now will matter. Paying your debts on time ensures there are no missed or late payments coming up in the next seven years.

Remember that credit history and the amount you owe is more important than the length of the history, new credit, and types of credit. While this strategy has been published by many people, it is generally accepted that in the 1950s and 1960s, Tony Capaldi was the first do describe how the credit bureaus worked. He emphasized the importance of maintaining a non-delinquent credit history. It was only negative items that would be reported at the time.

Today is different. Everything is reported today as a way to offer fair credit information and ratings. It is also the reason that paying your debts on time will help improve your credit history; therefore, your credit score.

It is never too late to start paying your debts on time. If you have suffered a financial setback such as a bankruptcy or poor payment history, without the need for bankruptcy, just start going back to paying your debts on time.

How the Strategy Works

- Set up automatic payments for all debts, when possible.
- Use a calendar, either a desk or an easily accessible calendar to mark when bills are due.
- Pay all bills three days or two weeks in advance of the due date depending on the bill type.

This strategy works on the budget concept. You are able to make the payments on time because you have a very strict budget. You have allotted for when your income arrives in your bank account and when you need to pay your bills.

It also works by setting up payments in advance, at least three days prior to the actual due date to account for any weekend, or any delay in payment acceptance. For example, if you have an IRS debt with an installment agreement, you cannot try to pay on the same day as stated in the agreement. It doesn't work.

Even the IRS requires more than a few hours to process payments. It is far better to give a lead time of a week to make the payment if you are setting up payments via ACH to ensure they come out on the right day.

Automatic ACH payments will be drawn on the day you set them up, which makes it the company's responsibility to withdraw on the day you specified. However, if the payment is ACH, but you go in to set it up each month, you have to provide lead time. It may not make sense, but you have undoubtedly seen the blacked out dates, such as the day you are trying to make a payment due to the lead time issue.

For individuals who still send checks to certain companies, you want at least two weeks' lead time.

Budgeting for on time Payments

- Know when your money is coming in.
- Set all your bills around your income versus the due dates.
- Pay everything you can for the month, while leaving yourself fuel, grocery, and miscellaneous money for expenditures.

If you set your bills around receiving your income you are more apt to pay the bills on time, not spend the money you need for the bills, and improve your credit history.

Your credit history will only improve over time and based on when your creditor will report to the company. Most companies report every three to four months versus each month. Some companies will average what has occurred rather than attempt to put in every little detail.

If you are late one out of three months, then you might not see a ding to your credit at all. However, if you are continuously late or missing payments, then it is reported as accurately as possible.

The way reporting occurs gives you a chance to improve your credit history over time by consistently being on time with your payments and ensuring that the old late/missed payments fall off.

Key Points

- Set up as many payments as possible for automatic withdrawal.
- Have the funds removed at least three days before the bill being due or two days after you receive your income.
- Pay your bills first, then budget for groceries, fuel, and incidentals.

Automatic Payments Equal Consistency

Automatic ACH Payments Provide Reliability

Yes, there are still some accounts you don't want to get paid automatically. Utilities that change each month can affect your budget. If you don't have the money, then your bank account can suddenly get an overdrawn fee, which makes it much harder to pay your debts. One way to counteract this is a properly budget as previously discussed. For the accounts that you do not mind setting up automatic payments, it is imperative that you do so. To be considered reliable and consistent, you need to reflect that image by setting up accounts that you don't have to worry.

But, what about safety? It is a primary concern. You may also be asking yourself—what if I think I will have the money, but I end up not having it? The key to automatic payments is found in budgeting, but also understanding your financial limitations. Technology has helped us in so many ways with regard to payment consistency and reliability.

ACH payments started to blossom in the mid-2000s, when it was seen that the internet could truly be a tool for numerous things. However, it was not until the last six to eight years that more people have become comfortable with automatic payments.

Quite a few of the older generation are still not certain they should set up automatic payments or let their credit card information be known online. Around 2009, more secure measures were added. These measures for setting up automatic payments have become even better in the last five years.

This strategy is not so much about the improvement to your credit score that ACH automatic payments can offer you, as it is about gaining a side benefit. The side benefit is the reliability and consistency in your credit history, which does offer you an increase in your credit score. However, the true meaning of the strategy is to be safe while you are using automatic payments.

How it Works

- On all accounts, where you can set up automatic withdrawals, do so.

- Set the payment to come out three days after your income is directly deposited or deposited into your account.

- Make the agreed payment for the month, in full.

- When possible, utilize online payment options that hide your identity.

Some credit accounts require your checking account information. However, other accounts are allowing you to use a secure account ID. You can set up a credit card number that is used only for online transactions, where a hacker is unable to access the credit card holder's information. PayPal and other online methods of payment can also be used for secure transactions without your personal checking account information being spread. Some places treat PayPal transfers as direct deposits.

Key Points

For this strategy, you are paying on time with your automatic payments, but you are also going a step further in setting up a means to keep your identity more hidden from potential hackers. If you have ever had your accounts misused or your identity stolen, then you know how detrimental it can be to your credit history and scores. You might not have been the one to make the mess, but you still have to live with the damage. Utilizing other methods of payment that keep your identity secure, while also setting up automatic payments for those credit accounts is one strategy you might wish to employ.

It is a newer option and less well known. Whenever possible pay with a credit card or online account that provides you with a number to use once or to use as a way to hide your checking account information for automatic payments. Bank of America also provides a safe shop system which adds an extra layer of protection when you shop online. It generates a temporary credit card number that links directly to your real credit card account number. Your card number remains completely private and protected.

Secured Credit Card

Establish Credit History with Money you have

The usage of a secured credit card for raising your credit score is another new millennium concept. Stephen Snyder, Credit Karma, and Credit.com all discuss the use of a secured credit card to improve your credit score.

A secured credit card is different from the typical credit card because you put money into an account, and only that money can be used to make purchases. A regular credit card provides you with a credit limit, and you can spend until you reach that credit limit.

The credit bureaus also treat secured and unsecured credit cards the same way with regard to your credit score. The bureaus and FICO look at when the card was opened, the limit you have on it, the balance, and the payment history. If you allow the card to sit unused, empty, and still open, this can actually have a negative effect on your credit.

The negative effect comes from the fees usually associated with having the secured credit card. Most companies offering secured cards have an annual fee, which has to be paid. The payment will come off of your credit deposit each year, just like the annual fee on a regular credit card is tacked onto the credit balance you have.

If you use secured credit cards correctly, you can start building a better credit history with an appropriate debt ratio. The debt ratio is based on how much income you report versus how much debt you have. You'll discover later there is a strategy that can be used to build a better credit history.

For now, understand that it is better to have a secured credit card with $500 as the balance, where you use only $100 each month versus using the entire $500 and putting another $500 on the card for the next month.

How Secured Credit Cards Work

- Search around for the best secured credit card. Depending on your current credit history, you may be able to gain one without an annual fee.

- Examine the security deposit you need to put down for the card. Unlike prepaid credit cards, which exist, the secured credit card does not, always, require the same deposit amount as the credit limit. For example, if you have a credit limit from Capital One for $200, you may be asked for a security deposit of $49. It is based on your creditworthiness.

- The security deposit is held in an account and not typically used when you use the card to clear the balance. Instead, you have a monthly payment to make. If you use the $200 limit, then you owe $200 for that month.

- Many secured credit cards will raise your credit line after a period of time where you do not require further deposits. In other words, if in the first 5 months of having the card, you make use of the card, make a payment for the amount spent, and do not use any of your deposit, your credit limit may increase.

The key to these cards is that you are making a monthly payment just as you are with a regular credit card. The only difference is that you need to provide a certain security deposit based on your credit history. The advantage is that these cards report to the credit bureaus.

Secured credit cards often get mistaken for prepaid credit cards. Prepaid credit cards are items you can pick up in a retail store, load money on them, and use them like a Visa or MasterCard. Many "gift cards" that are sent out by retailers are prepaid cards so that you can use them as a credit card, with a certain amount prepaid money. Since prepaid cards do not have an account associated with them, they are not reported to the credit bureau.

Secured credit cards do have an account. You open it like a credit card, use it as a credit card, but you have secured it with a deposit like you secure a mortgage with your home's value.

How the Strategy Works

- Open a secured credit card account.
- Make the security deposit.
- Use the card for fuel or other small purchases, at least once a month.
- Go home and make a payment to the card for the purchase made.
- The credit card will report your account "in good standing."
- You need to keep the purchases on the lower 50 percent of the credit card limit.

- It needs to be paid off each month, ensuring you do not touch your deposit.
- As long as you are reported "in good standing," your credit score will increase over time.

Key Points

Secured credit cards like all other strategies in this book are not miracle solutions. It takes time for the creditor to report your account history and for this history to be calculated as part of your overall score. The more "good standing" credit you have, the higher your credit score will be.

Enjoying your eBook so far? Take a moment to subscribe to our FREE newsletter for incredible discounts, books giveaways, and VIP offers!

> http://www.connectionbooksclub.com/bonus/

All we need is your email, and you'll be set up to receive more of the eBooks you can't wait to read.

Attach to a Family Account

Building or Rebuilding Your Credit through the Family

Are you just starting out? Perhaps you just graduated high school and are headed off to college? The first thing you are probably going to do towards building your credit history is take out student loans. Student loans are not weighted heavily when it comes to your credit history. They are installment agreements, but until you start paying for them or pay them off in full, they are not considered a good indication of personal credit history.

There are a couple of reasons for this that will be brought up later on, in a chapter dedicated to student loans. The point is that through the use of credit cards you can build credit, but as a newly graduated 17 or 18 years old, it will be extremely tough for you to get a decent credit card. Companies will offer you credit lines, but with higher interest rates and lower credit limits. Building credit as a young person, you want to have good interest rates in the event you do use the card and only make a minimum payment. It is also helpful to have a higher limit than you ever intend on using because of the credit utilization ratio.

Two things will make you look good when you are new to credit building: paying off the account each month and having a high limit you never reach.

Individuals who are rebuilding credit will also run into the same issues as those trying to establish their credit. You will discover no one wants to give you a good interest rate, and you will only be given a small credit limit if you can even get a line of credit.

The issues of finding affordable credit to utilize are not as important as finding a company willing to give you credit and a decent credit limit. You want the amount you owe to be small, but when other companies see you are being given high credit limits, it is often easier to get new credit.

Using family to obtain credit is by far the oldest strategy in existence, in terms of building credit. When credit scores became emphasized in our culture as highly important, the usage of family accounts to increase your score to gain more or better credit offers became common.

How it Works

- Determine if a family member is willing to sign you on as an authorized user of their account and provide you with a credit card in your name.

- If you are tied to another account, in name and with a credit card number assigned to you, the information will be reported to your credit report.

- You will need to keep the account at a zero balance, if possible. This strategy works best if you have a zero account balance each month.

- If you cannot get a zero balance, then make sure you are keeping the credit balance below the 30% mark for the credit limit. Basically, if you are given a card with $500 as the credit limit, you should never let that card be over $150.

- Keep the credit account open, in use, and paid off.

Having the account will show that you are establishing credit. By keeping it paid on time and in use, you are showing that you can pay the card and are consistent with those payments. If you don't use the card, it is not going to help you build credit. There is nothing to report other than an unused card. Some companies might report this as "good standing," most will not even bother.

In fact, if you open an account, but never use it, you can see "no history to report," instead of "good" or "late payment."

An Alternative Option

Credit cards can be dangerous. You have a limit, but you are also tempted to spend up to that limit. For younger generations, this can be especially difficult. They may have trouble stopping their spending because they think of just one little item, until it adds up to be a lot of money owed.

Another way to build credit without the danger of revolving credit, is through a car loan. Here is how it works:

- You, as the younger generation, will save up money from having a steady job.
- You will amass enough to either pay for a car outright over a period of one year or a sizeable down payment to help lower the monthly payment. It will take time, but if you are serious about owning a car, then saving $5,000 working part-time from the time you are 16, will ensure you have at least that much. Even a couple of summers working full time can provide you with a good down payment for a vehicle. This strategy also

works well for those that are much older and still don't have a credit history or bad credit history.

- Bring your parent to a bank to help obtain the car loan. The bank will see that you have no credit history and assess the cosigner's credit history. An interest rate will be determined. If the interest rate is affordable, below 5 percent, the strategy will be slightly different.

- For an interest rate below 5%, you are going to pay the loan off in two years. Yes, you are going to spend a little more because you are paying interest. However, it is the consistency of the payment being on time combined with the length of the loan that will help you build credit. Furthermore, when you finally pay the loan off in full, you will show that you are reliable.

- If the interest rate is less than desirable, anything over 5%, then you are going to pay it off within a year. You will still make payments for a few months to show that you were on top of the payment requirements of the installment agreement, but then you will pay everything off. It is not going to help your score as much as keeping the line open longer. However, you are going to show that you had the capability of paying it off in full, as well as the ability to lower the amount owed.

With this strategy, you want to show that you had savings, as well as the ability to make on-time payments. You also want to ensure you are not entering into a situation that would harm you financially. Paying high interest can become a burden versus helping you.

There is another way you can utilize this car loan strategy to build credit when you are young. You have the option of paying on a loan with high interest and tied to a family member, for a year, then approaching banks for a new car loan. State you want to get the loan under your name, so you would like to refinance, as well as obtain a significantly lower interest rate.

If the deal is not worth the refinancing costs, do not go for it. If it is worth the refinancing fees, then get the loan into your name, at a lower interest rate, and benefit from a longer payment history. You will also benefit from showing that it is solely in your name versus tied to another. When you build a credit history, companies look at whether or not you have a long history, but also at how you obtained the loans. Someone who is not qualified to obtain a loan on their own will not be considered a person with "great" credit.

Key Points

- This strategy works for new credit creators and those rebuilding credit.
- You need to tie to a family account to be accepted and find a decent interest rate/credit limit.
- You can use other lines of credit versus a credit card.

The most used form of creating and building credit for younger generations and those rebuilding their credit is credit cards. However, it doesn't have to be this way. You don't have to depend solely on credit cards as a way to use this strategy. Any line of credit you can obtain, like a car loan, mortgage, or a personal line of credit will help you increase your credit score, as well as build credit. The point is you are using a type of credit that you can afford to build consistency in your credit history.

Get an Increased Limit

Working the Debt Amount Owed

The second most important percentage FICO uses to assess your creditworthiness and thus determine your credit score is "amount owed." The more you owe, without a savings account to pay it all off—the lower your credit score is going to be. It is a debt to income ratio concept. You can have a very high credit limit on numerous open accounts, but when you start to owe closer to all of those credit limits, your scores decrease.

If you have a situation where you are edging closer to the credit limit or the perfect credit utilization ratio, then you will want to see about getting a credit limit increase. Some credit card companies will notice you are getting closer to the limit and assess your credit history.

For individuals that are not in arrears, it is possible for you to get an increased credit limit, automatically. The company will just increase the limit without asking you.

Some credit accounts will increase your limit if you ask. It will depend on your standing with the company.

How it Works

- Call the company.
- Ask that they review your credit card account.
- State that you make on-time payments and you simply want to improve your credit scores.

- If you can, state that you are willing to make an increased payment right then and there on the phone as a promise that you are paying the card down.

- You may need to speak with an account manager with higher permissions than the individual that first answers. If you do need this approval, ask for it. Don't take no for an answer from the customer service representative that answers the phone. There is nothing wrong with asking to speak with a supervisor to get what you want, as long as you make it clear that the person who answered was very helpful, they just didn't have the same permissions.

As with any of the strategies throughout this book, you need to understand that your score is not going to increase two seconds after you gain the credit limit increase. It is a tool to help you get better scores in the next few months. When FICO reassesses your credit scores, then you will see a change in your score from all the changes you are making to build a better credit history.

Key Points

- Increasing your credit limit is not so you spend more on your credit cards.

- The increase in your limit is designed to increase your score because you have a higher limit than the debt amount owed.

- If you spend more because you have a higher limit, then nothing is going to change.

- It will also require time for your scores to increase.

- The increase is not going to be hundreds of points, but a steady increase.

- Use this strategy as you gain independent accounts from family too. If you have credit being built on old family accounts, then you can switch to your own account and ask for an increase in your credit limit.

The more strategies you utilize to make your credit look better, the more your score will increase over time. You may only gain 5 points with a credit limit increase, but at least this is five more points to your credit score than before.

Multiple Monthly Payments

Payment consistency and debt reduction, increase your scores

There has never been a time when multiple monthly payments were bad for your credit score and credit "appearance." However, financial experts started pushing the multiple payment strategy in the last 8 years when several people started suffering from financial setbacks.

It was determined that people had to learn that their high debt was killing their scores. For those with the means to correct their situation quickly, making multiple monthly payments started to seem like one of the best strategies available for credit repair.

It is not the multiple payment that makes a big deal. You are only reported as having made the payment on time or "missed/late" with payments. So the frequency, in this respect doesn't matter.

In fact, you could make a huge payment once a month to your credit accounts and still increase your credit score, just as making two payments will increase your score. It is about reducing the amount you owe that helps increase your overall credit score.

There is another factor to consider in making more payments. You may not be able to learn when your creditor reports your payment history. Some companies report your credit history once a month, but that may be mid-cycle. If you make a payment mid-cycle, then you are reported in good standing. If you accidentally fall between the reporting cycle for the month with your last month's payment and the new month's payment, you could be miss-reported to the bureaus. You want to look favorable, always.

How it Works

- Set up an automatic payment to come out on or around the due date.

- In the middle of the month or a few weeks after your typical payment, set up a second payment.

- If you can, make a payment each week to the credit account.

Keeping on top of payments is not only helpful for building your credit score back up, but it helps you keep to a routine to ensure that you are never going to miss or make a late payment again.

Key Points

- This works for revolving accounts.

- It can also work on installment agreements.

- By making more payments you are reducing the "amount owed."

- It is not to show more consistency in payments.

This strategy is particularly helpful for individuals who tend to miss payments or make late payments each month. When you get into a routine to pay more frequently, the debt is always on your mind. You will stop missing those payment dates because you are striving towards a goal of making the debt smaller, more quickly.

Enjoying your eBook so far? Take a moment to subscribe to our FREE newsletter for incredible discounts, books giveaways, and VIP offers!

- http://www.connectionbooksclub.com/bonus/

All we need is your email, and you'll be set up to receive more of the eBooks you can't wait to read.

Keep Old Credit Accounts Open

Utilize the length of credit in the calculation

Remember that after seven years you can remove delinquent or negative credit information. So, why would you want to keep old credit accounts open, if you don't see a use for them anymore? As we have been going through the first ten strategies to build great credit and increase your credit scores, the FICO calculation has been consistently mentioned.

You know that payment history is weighted the most, with the amount owed weighted at 30% of the overall calculation. The length of time you have had a credit account may only impact your score between 10 and 15 percent, but that is still a factor in the overall calculation.

New accounts are also part of the overall calculation. When they happen frequently, they can hinder your credit as opposed to helping it. For instance, if you needed a new utility account three times in the same year that is going to hurt your credit versus having the same utility company for 30 years. The person switching utility companies three times in the same year is seen as unstable. There must be a reason for them to be moving around. There may be a legitimate reason, but typically moving around a lot is a sign of not being able to afford where you currently live in as opposed to something like finding a new job, buying a new house, etc.

Even if you are not going to use certain accounts with a high frequency, you still want to keep them open. Installment agreements will end, and open accounts like utilities will be closed when you move. So, this strategy is best for checking, savings, retirement accounts, and credit cards.

Although opening and closing a savings or checking account does not have a significant effect on your credit score, any violations of the bank's account agreement could show up on a consumer report known as the ChexSystems report. The ChexSystems report records any violations from bank accounts, not credit accounts.

Repeated opening and closing of accounts to take advantage of sign-up offers may be recorded on your ChexSystems report. Excessive withdrawals from savings and money market accounts, unpaid overdraft fees and negative account balances are other examples of other violations that can are recorded. Bank can reject your checking or saving account application if you have many violations.

How it Works

- Do not close old credit card accounts.
- Use the card once a month.
- Pay off the amount you have put on the card.
- By paying off the card each month, you are not going to pay interest.

This strategy is fairly simple. You do not want to close old credit card accounts. From time to time, such as one time each month, you need to use the card, and then pay it off.

Key Points

- You are not going to pay interest as long as the balance is paid in full.
- Make sure to use the card for at least one transaction in the month, but a transaction you know you can pay off.
- Each time you use the card and pay it off, you are showing that you are consistent and reliable. You will be reported as "in good standing."
- If you do not use the card, it will not help you increase your score.
- It will help show that you have an old credit history.

Your bank accounts also lend to a steadiness of life. They matter to the "length of credit," part of the calculation. Someone who has the same bank accounts for six decades has a better score than the person who decided to close and open these types of accounts three or four times in a two-year time frame. There may be reasons for it, such as better fees with a different bank. You do want to make your financial situation better, but if at all possible, keeping your first bank account open is a good thing.

Have Multiple Credit Types

Multiple types of credit help you show a well-rounded credit portfolio

The types of credit you have will weigh less in your credit score calculation since it is only 10% of the score. However, that 10% still matters. If you have only credit cards, then you show a financial institution that you know how to use revolving debt. But, it does nothing to show your consistency with a long-term loan that is "paid in full."

Installment agreements, when paid in full, are highly favorable because they show that for a certain period, you stuck with the monthly payment, and then paid it off on time or early. Financial companies look at this history in a favorable light.

Open credit accounts are used in the calculation to show that you can make a monthly payment for services rendered and that you have consistently been at the same address or utilizing the same account for years. It is the length of time and payment history that matter with open accounts.

Revolving credit does help, but you have to use it correctly. If you carry a balance, that will be shown. If you have a high balance, consistently, on the card, then it can look less favorable than a low balance with on time payments. Better yet, if you use the card each month and pay it off before the next cycle, you look even better.

Open accounts and revolving credit show a length of credit. They also show consistent payments over the decades you may have the accounts. This also weighs into your score and whether you have "great credit."

When credit became more desirable, and the credit bureaus began figuring out score calculations, and as soon as FICO became known, this strategy of having more than one type of credit was established in the 1970s.

How it Works

- Have at least one revolving credit account.
- Have at least one installment account.
- Have at least one open credit account.
- Make monthly payments to each account, if possible pay off the balance.
- Only leave a balance on the installment account, such as a car loan or mortgage, as these are usually larger credit accounts that you need several years to pay off.

The payment history, amount owed, and length of the account being open weigh higher, but types of credit can also increase or decrease your score. Too many credit cards work against you as opposed to installment accounts when paid on time will benefit you.

Key Points

- You want multiple credit types to show a well-rounded credit history.
- The credit type does factor into your score.
- Installment agreements such as student loans are weighted differently than car loans.

- The more installment agreements you pay off, the better it is for your credit history and score.
- You want consistency in open accounts to show a longer history, i.e. moving less, more stability in your life, and reliability.

Pay Debt as You Go

Pay off accounts in full each month to increase your scores

When you only spend what you can afford, then your credit usage is low, you can make on time payments, and you increase your credit scores. Financial health and great credit work on the ability to actually afford things. People who have plenty of savings can still have poor scores because they have a high usage ratio.

People with plenty of money and the ability to pay off their debts in full, who pay off credit cards each month, will have better scores. If you want to be this latter type of person, then you need to live within your means and pay your debts as you go.

It is not a new strategy at all. People used to pay off their debts each month, avoid most credit cards, and live within their means. In the 80s and 90s credit card usage started to increase, where it became acceptable to have credit card debt. There was still the general thought that the debt would not max out the cards and it would be paid off slowly or in a large chunk at the end of the year.

Somehow between the old and new millennium, credit card debt became the norm, where you didn't have to pay it off right away. But, this belief did not help your credit. Great credit comes from a low debt ratio, where you make on time monthly payments, have old accounts, a few new accounts, and various types of credit. If you can establish a good looking credit report, then your scores will naturally be in the higher ranges.

How it Works

- Pay off your credit card balance each month.
- Pay your utilities and other open accounts in full each month.
- Make more than the monthly payment for installment agreements.

You don't have to pay off installment agreements as quickly as revolving credit. The fact is they are often too large to do so, but you can make more of a monthly payment as a way to be consistent, reliable, and lower the debt owed for a more favorable outlook.

Key Points

- Paying off the debt as you go lowers your debt ratio compared to your income.
- You want a favorable debt to income ratio to gain new lines of credit.
- You have more financial stability because you are only spending what you can afford versus over spending.
- Paying more to your installment agreements also means less interest paid out.
- Your scores go up with "paid in full" accounts versus high debt, open accounts.

Utilizing the system by paying as you go and affording the debts you have, ensures you can get better loans, credit cards, and interest rates. These better products ensure great credit, with high credit scores.

Enjoying your eBook so far? Take a moment to subscribe to our FREE newsletter for incredible discounts, books giveaways, and VIP offers!

> ➢ http://www.connectionbooksclub.com/bonus/

All we need is your email, and you'll be set up to receive more of the eBooks you can't wait to read.

Credit Utilization Ratio

A credit utilization ratio is a calculation of how much debt you have versus your credit limit

The credit utilization ratio is calculated by looking at your credit limits and determining how much of the limit you have used. If you have $500 on a credit card and you used $400, then your usage of the card is high. This negatively impacts your credit score because of the high amount of debt. If you have three credit cards, and the other two are below the 50% usage mark, it looks more favorable, than if you have all three cards maxed out.

In the first decade of the millennium, it was highly publicized by bankruptcy experts and financial gurus like Stephen Snyder, Motley Fool writers, and others that you need to have your debt below 30% of your credit limit. In other words, all revolving credit accounts should be at 29% maximum of the credit limit in order to increase your credit score.

In this strategy, it is about the amount you owe versus the payment history. Yes, payment history matters, but the idea is behind this strategy is to focus on the amount owed, while maintaining correct monthly payments.

How it Works

- Maintain a balance that is at least 71% below your credit limit.

- Record how much you are charging to each revolving credit account.

- Have balance alerts set up.
- Obtain a credit limit increase.
- Determine when your creditor reports to the bureaus.
- Pay mid-cycle to your card to show an extra payment for the 30-day cycle.

The quicker you can pay down debts the better for this strategy to work on your credit score.

Key Points

- The amount of credit you have and the amount you utilize can determine your credit score.
- If you use more of your credit, meaning you are above the 30% mark, your credit score will decrease.
- A lower credit utilization ensures your credit score will increase or at least stay the same.
- By using this strategy, you know when to make payments to reflect well on your credit report.
- You are also lowering your credit utilization ratio with additional payments.

Yes, the consistent and increased payments help in this strategy, but remember the focus is to get your revolving debts below the 30% mark to help increase your scores.

Keep "Credit" Below 30% Income

You want a low debt to income ratio for better scores

If you have a high amount of debt, you already know that your credit scores will be less than a person with a low amount of debt paying on time just as you are. The key is to ensure that you look financially sound, but if you have a lot of debt, then you start getting score deductions because there is a potential of you starting to miss your payments. The financial formula may be unknown for FICO scores, but there is also a general thought process behind lenders guidelines. They are willing to provide loans, lines of credit and credit cards as long as you have a good payment history, pay off debts in full, and keep a low credit usage.

When you rebuild your credit history, such as after a bankruptcy, it was discovered that if you could get your debts below the 30% income ratio, then your scores would increase quicker than a person with a remaining high debt.

In the financial world, it has always been important to keep your debt lower than 50% of your income as a means of financial health and making payments. It was in the mid-2000s, and definitely around 2008 that gurus like Snyder began pushing the concept of a debt to income ratio, where your debt is less than 30% of your yearly income.

If you make $50,000 a year, then you want your debt to be no higher than $15,000 because it shows that your credit usage is affordable, and you still have income to pay off new debts should you need a new loan.

How it Works

- Determine where you stand with "credit"
- If possible, pay off debts to lower your credit usage to below 30% of what you make.
- Set up to keep 20% of your income in savings.
- Reduce your monthly mortgage or rental fee to less than 50% of your monthly income.
- Cut expenses where you can to reduce your credit usage.

It will take time to cut expenses and to reduce the debt amount you have. However, it is imperative for building a better credit report.

Key Points

- The more savings you have, the more favorable you look to creditors.
- There is a potential to increase your credit limit to obtain a better credit utilization ratio.
- You are living within your means, which means less potential to make late payments or missed payments.
- Your score will increase because you have a favorable debt to income ratio.
- Your credit history will be more dependable because you are making on-time payments.
- You will find more products open to you, at better interest rates.

You want to look favorable to creditors. One of the best ways for this to happen is by ensuring that your credit usage is 29% or less of your income. You also want to ensure that your credit health looks good, so your score calculation will increase.

Seek Credit Unions

Credit unions offer exclusive member products that could help your debt situation

Starting accounts like checking or savings accounts that are new will not look as favorably as having one account for the last 30 years. However, the benefits you gain from credit unions make it worth starting a new account that will have money in it. Even a couple of hundred dollars in a savings account reflect better for your credit history and scores.

Better still is the access you gain to member only products, such as better credit card offers or loans. Certain credit unions require you to be requested into them, while others let you in if you meet certain qualifications. It is far better to be asked to join because you are a desired customer. This also originates from having great credit.

The use of credit unions has often been about finding affordable products. It is only in the last couple of years that websites like Motley Fool, Huffington Post, and others have stated that credit unions are a good place to open accounts. There are drawbacks since there are usually fees associated with the accounts. Some do not let you withdraw or make payments to the account as freely as you can with a non-credit union. Despite some disadvantages, you gain more by establishing better credit history.

This strategy works best if you only open a checking or savings, or both of those accounts with the credit union versus loan or credit card. The new account will become old, and help lend to your stability. However, you can also use a loan or a credit card to increase your score. Keeping a low credit usage allows you to improve your history, as well as your score.

How it Works

- Open a savings or checking account with a credit union.
- Apply for a loan or credit card.
- Make payments to the loan or credit card.

The payments, low amount owed, and new credit will help you build a good financial picture.

Key Points

- Credit Unions are for members.
- Becoming a member of a credit union can be difficult depending on which one you approach. The tougher it is to be a member, the better. You want to be sought for your business.
- There are member products that you can get at better rates than the average person. These affordable products help you build a credit history.

While not weighted as more important in the scheme of "great" credit usage, if you are a member of an exclusive credit union, it can weigh more heavily at a different financial institution. It won't help your score, other than to provide you with a new credit history, amount owed, and fulfil the other three points of how your score is calculated, as a means of gaining a better credit score.

Enjoying your eBook so far? Take a moment to subscribe to our FREE newsletter for incredible discounts, books giveaways, and VIP offers!

- http://www.connectionbooksclub.com/bonus/

All we need is your email, and you'll be set up to receive more of the eBooks you can't wait to read.

Paying Off Installment Accounts

Paid in full accounts look great to financial companies

Financial companies such as car loan lenders, mortgage brokers, and other installment accounts like to see that you do not have a high amount of debt and that you pay off your accounts as agreed.

This strategy started being publicized more with the mortgage crisis in the late 2000s. In the strategy you are asked to continue making on time monthly payments to all debts, but to use the savings you have to pay off installment accounts. Overall, it frees up that monthly payment to be allocated elsewhere. More importantly, when you pay off an account you look better financially due to the reduced amount owed and paying as agreed.

Like other strategies mentioned in the book, this one is tied specifically to credit utilization and a steady, consistent credit history for a better overall score.

How it Works

- Pay the account each month.
- When you have saved enough, pay off the account.
- Try to pay off the account before the end date of the installment agreement.

Making more payments or paying a lump sum to "pay in full," is a great way to reduce the amount owed and show that you can pay your accounts in full as agreed.

Key Points

- By paying the account in full, your debt utilization decreases.

- You have completed an agreement, which appears favorable.

- Your score will increase because you have paid the debt, without arrears.

- The account will remain on your credit history showing "good standing" and paid in full.

Your credit score is going to increase whenever you have less owed. You are also going to establish a better payment history that makes you look like you have great credit. You are showing that you have a decent income, as well as a lower overall debt ratio to that income. Lenders like this, particularly, if you are trying to get a mortgage. Great credit comes from great scores, but also the stability of the debt you do have.

Chapter 17: Pay Off Debt

Using consolidation or settlement strategies to pay down debts

Already it has been discussed that if you pay off your debts as you go or pay more towards them, it will help you build a better credit history and increase your score. Paying off your debts in this chapter provides you with a strategy that might help you get rid of some debts faster for the overall health of your credit report.

Like many strategies, you have had the option of settling your debts with companies for decades. Lenders always want as much money as you can give them versus being shafted for the entire amount in a bankruptcy. It is just that consolidation and settlement options rose in popularity during the recent financial crisis making it appear in more articles and news pieces than ever before.

If you have savings to pay off your debts, then start with the most expensive. Otherwise, utilize settlement options where you are able to reduce the amount owed if you pay a certain amount right now. As long as the account shows paid in full, with a strong payment history, your scores are going to increase. It doesn't matter if you needed to use debt settlement strategies to make the debt end. It just matters that you have paid the debt off instead of letting it go into arrears.

How it Works

- Determine what debts you can pay off.
- Make a payment to pay off as many debt accounts as possible.
- Use credit settlement strategies if necessary.
- Your scores will increase as you reduce the amount of debt owed.

Consolidation can also be an option, where you put all your debts into one loan, as a means of paying off all the other loans with "good standing" and ensuring you can make the monthly payment on time.

Key Points

- Paying off debt is best for your financial situation.
- Decreasing what you owe increases your potential for making on time payments.
- Paid in full accounts look good to lending companies.
- Your scores will slowly start to increase, as reporting companies and FICO recalculate those scores.

The point is to get debts paid off. Even if the amount owed is not reduced right away, the fact that accounts are showing paid off reflects good on your credit report. It will factor into whether you can get new lines of credit later on, as well as help increase your score. As long as you make payments to the consolidation account, your score will continue to be at the increased level. Furthermore, if you settle certain debts, it frees up money to be paid towards other debts, thus reducing the amount owed.

Lower Interest Rate Last

Make it feasible to pay down debts, so you continue working on credit repair

Several bankruptcy gurus, including Stephen Snyder, tell you to pay off the lower interest rate debts last, unless you can consolidate all your debt to that one credit account. It is not a new strategy, but it did resurface in the mid-2000s with all the credit troubles, and is going strong in the newest decade.

The higher the interest rate on a credit account, the more you are paying in interest each month. This can strain you financially. Rather than allowing it to continue, you have to figure out a way to reduce your amount owed, make on time monthly payments, and repair your credit or build your credit history in a better light.

The way to do that is by utilizing a strategy that keeps the lower interest rate around longer and gets rid of the ones that are straining you financially. The good news is you can also use consolidation by moving money around.

The key is to have a good credit utilization ratio, so it doesn't mean each of your credit accounts needs to be below 50%, but that your overall ratio is low compared to your income.

Yes, it helps if all accounts are below 50%, but when you are working to reduce the amount owed, you need to use everything available, which means reducing the interest you pay out, to increase the principal amount you are paying. It is why you want to reduce your interest rates, if at all possible, as well as increase credit limits on credit accounts with better APRs.

How it Works

- Start paying off your debts with on time monthly payments.

- Create a budget that is "debt minded."

- Using your budget, pay extra income towards the debt with the highest interest rate.

- Keep the credit cards or loans with the lower interest rates for last.

To a point this strategy works on budget like others mentioned in this book. It just helps build on the concept that if you have a budget, then you can allocate funds to debts that need to be lowered. Once you have all your debts paid off, you keep the accounts open because the long term account helps with your score. It also helps to use it once a month, pay it off in full, and build your score and history in this manner.

Key Points

- Paying off your debts increases your score.

- By paying off higher interest rates first, you are paying out less in interest over time.

- Since you are getting rid of the more expensive debts first, you are freeing up money to pay off your debts quicker in the coming years.

- This strategy works on the premise that you are attempting to maintain a good credit history, while making it financially feasible to lower your overall debt amount.

Great credit is built on having a good credit payment history, a low amount owed, and a long term credit history versus new debts. This strategy just makes it possible for you to pay down your debts faster, while benefiting from an increase in score with each account you pay off in full.

Enjoying your eBook so far? Take a moment to subscribe to our FREE newsletter for incredible discounts, books giveaways, and VIP offers!

- http://www.connectionbooksclub.com/bonus/

All we need is your email, and you'll be set up to receive more of the eBooks you can't wait to read.

Lower Balance First

Paying the lowest balance off first gives you confidence

Credit repair is about reducing the amount of financial debt you have. There are two reasons to ensure you are reducing your financial obligations: to become debt free and to repair your credit. Given how these two things go hand in hand, it is important to speak about both here.

Robert Kiyosaki, Stephen Snyder, and other financial gurus tell you that you want to make your money work for you as a means of better financial health. It is true. But, when you are in a high debt situation, it can look bleak. You might be at a loss of what to pay off or whether it will actually help your credit.

Anytime you reduce the amount you owe, with on time monthly payments or pay off an account in full, you are going to get a boost in your credit scores. Secondly, you are going to reduce your financial burden and free up funds to pay off other debts.

Starting with the lowest balance first became popular in the mid-2000s when hundreds of spun articles started hitting the internet about becoming "debt free." It is not a new concept, but the strategy of how it works has been given new "light."

You are told to pay off the lowest balance first as a means of boosting your confidence that you can become debt free. If you pay off one account, then it becomes easier to pay off another and another, until you no longer have a high balance of debt owed.

How it Works
- Start with a goal to pay off your debts.
- To reach this goal set up a way to pay the lowest balance first.
- Make increased payments to that debt, until it is paid in full.
- If the lower balance is also the lower interest rate, pay it off.
- Once the debt is paid off, do a balance transfer to the revolving credit account, assuming it is one, and start paying off a new balance.

Key Points
- Paying off the lower balance first is for your budget and your conscience. If you can reach a goal of getting a debt paid off, then you can feel stronger about your financial situation. The strategy will also help with building a better credit report and scores.
- Debts paid in full look appealing to lenders.
- Lower debt utilization means better scores.
- Decreased debt frees up more income to make payments on time.
- You still have the benefit of a credit history, just with a better outlook than before.
- Moving your debt from one card to another helps you utilize better interest rates.

➢ It can also show that you are paying off an "account in full" such as a higher interest rate card, as well as the amount on the lower balance card. This boosts your score each time, you reduce the amount owed.

Remember, your credit payment history and amount owed weigh heavily in increasing your score, while length of credit accounts also matters. In this situation you are ensuring that your credit report has a decent history of payments and a reduction of the amount owed.

Student Loans and Scores

Why Student Loans Can Help and Hurt Scores

Discussing family accounts as a way to build credit, it was mentioned that people starting out will usually have student loans as their first credit account, unless they obtain a car loan or credit cards tied to a family member with credit history. Student loans are a tricky area of installment credit history because they are not looked on as favorably as you would imagine.

You might think that having opened student loan accounts when you first went to college would show a history of the account, but in actuality, only when you start making your first payment will student loans count as "credit payment history." Most student loans are in a deferred status as long as you are in school. Once you are out of school, you have one to four months before the companies begin asking you to make monthly payments that pay down the principal and interest.

Yet, when you have student loans, you have an "amount owed." This amount owed can actually be reducing your credit scores. One the one hand, you feel that making payments should increase your scores, but then you get dinged for having a high amount owed.

So what can you reasonably do about student loan debt? Do you want to pay it off right away?

According to people like Stephen Snyder and Robert Kiyosaki, if you have student loan debt, you want to leave it as the last items you pay off. It comes down to an IRS strategy. The history of this strategy has existed since student loans became necessary for people to go to college. The minute the IRS allowed you to use your student loan interest paid as a deduction is when this strategy came into being.

How it Works

- Each month you make a payment you pay interest and a little towards your principal, when you are newly paying on the account.
- When you file taxes, you are asked to enter the amount in student loan interest you paid.
- The amount paid is a deduction.
- During this same period, you are paying a little of the "amount owed," thus reducing your overall debt amount.
- You are also making payments, and as long as they are on time and the full monthly amount, you are helping your scores.
- When you get to a point in the loan, where you are barely making any interest payment at all towards the balance, pay off the debt.

Key Points

Student loans, when you first start taking them out appear on your credit report, but without any payment history. It is just an open installment account. The lack of payment history does not help your score, nor does it hurt it. The debt utilization ratio on the other hand will hurt your score a little.

It is due to having this debt that makes your score a little lower than if you had no debt at all.

If this is the only debt you have, then it is also considered "little to no debt," which also does not help when you are trying to get new loans to build your credit history.

When it comes time to make payments to the student loan companies as part of your installment agreement, you need to be on time and pay the monthly amount asked for. If possible, pay more than the monthly amount.

Paying interest helps lower your taxes owed. You want this deduction and the payment history. The deduction may be the only thing you have helping you get a tax refund. The payment history is also helping you increase your score, as the balance goes down.

There will come a point when you are going to pay off the debt in full. Do this when the deduction on your taxes is no longer significant. The reduction of debt owed will also help at this point. The reason behind this key point lies in the other credit you have built. You should be in your 30s or 40s, with a mortgage, credit cards, and other credit that weighs more significantly on your ability to get credit. You no longer need the payment history from the student loans. In fact, given the amount of debt you might have at this point, you want to reduce the "amount owed" you have overall.

Dear Reader,

Connection Books Club wants to thank you for the purchase of one of our many informative eBooks! We hope you enjoyed your purchase and we want to invite you to join our club.

When you subscribe to our FREE club, you'll receive regular newsletters and incredible discounts on our bestselling books! Connection Books Club makes reading easy, giving you the content you want, at a price you can't believe. All that it takes to enroll in our FREE book club is your email. We'll send you the latest business and personal development news and highlight the newest books that are ready for you to enjoy.

http://www.connectionbooksclub.com/bonus/

As part of your subscription, we're giving you a FREE download of one of our favorite eBooks, *Money Management: Learn How to Organize Your Financial Life and Invest in Your Future.* This eBook covers many financial situations, such as lowering interest rates and exploring options surrounding bankruptcy, helping you determine the best financial action for you.

Money management may be difficult for some people, but with your FREE copy of *Money Management: Learn How to Organize Your Financial Life and Invest in Your Future,* you'll learn the skills and information you need to make the best decisions to secure your financial future. The strategies contained in this eBook, designed for the everyday person, offering easy to follow steps and money saving tips.

Understanding money and how to make it works for you is important and with this eBook, you'll learn what you need to know to start building your financial security. Here are the top 5 reasons for reading *Money Management: Learn How to Organize Your Financial Life and Invest in Your Future*:

1. The strategies in this book are designed to help real people achieve their financial goals.
2. Explore different options for retirement.
3. Discover hacks for navigating the grocery store's subtle spending traps.
4. Inform yourself about how you might be able to get away with paying less than you owe on credit cards and other outstanding debts.
5. Experience a feeling of newfound freedom when you understand that you have every ability to live a life of financial stability.

➢ Get your copy here:
   http://www.connectionbooksclub.com/bonus/

The benefits of receiving this eBook for FREE are endless! Take control of your finances and start living the life you want.

By subscribing to Connection Books Club, not only will you get incredible discounts, our FREE welcome gift eBook, and a regular newsletter, but you'll also get the opportunity to receive FREE eBooks! Subscribers are invited to share reviews of the eBooks they've read, earning new titles at no cost! All it takes to enroll is your email.

http://www.connectionbooksclub.com/bonus/

Discounts and free eBooks are just a click away! Enter your email for VIP access to new books, incredible deals and money saving options, and even free giveaways! And don't forget, by signing up today for Connection Books Club, you'll receive the incredible eBook *Money Management: Learn How to Organize Your Financial Life and Invest in Your Future* for FREE!

Connection Books Club is excited to have you join our ranks of subscribers. We hope you enjoy your FREE eBook and all the great reading coming your way soon!

http://www.connectionbooksclub.com/bonus/

Wrap up: Credit Repair overview

Thank you again for purchasing this book!

I hope this book was able to help you with your needs and to satisfy your reading pleasures.

Now, you have the information that will help you build better credit and increase your credit score. Some of these strategies may not work for your situation or if you have already been employing them. Hopefully, you found a few new strategies to try and will be able to achieve the status you wish to have in your credit scores.

For those who have suffered a financial setback such as years in arrears or a bankruptcy, it will take time. It takes 10 years for a bankruptcy to leave your credit history and no longer affect you, regardless if someone provides you with good credit lines until then. It can take 10 years for you to get back up into the 800s if you had a bankruptcy and some will not make it because they are not utilizing credit building options as stated in this book.

Anyone who has not created a long history with numerous types of credit may also be having trouble gaining a score above 800. However, you have fewer steps to take to get your credit scores higher. It simply takes paying attention to the credit types you have, ensuring that you open new accounts, keep old accounts open, and establish a long history with consistent and reliable payments, as well as a small "amount owed" in comparison to your income and credit limits.

It is possible for you to have a decent credit score, more than decent, an excellent score if you are willing to work towards it. Utilize family to start to gain new credit lines, if necessary. Make certain that if you are paying for something that uses credit to build your score, by putting the funds in your account, and going home and paying that purchase off right away. It is only the steady, reliable, and consistent credit history that is going to offer a "great credit" appearance, as well as the higher scores.

Since you have the tools available to you now, there is no better time than to get started right away with building great credit and increasing those scores.

If you have enjoyed this book, I'd greatly appreciate if you could leave an honest review on Amazon.

Reviews are very important to us authors, and it only takes a minute to post.

Thank you

www.ingramcontent.com/pod-product-compliance
Lightning Source LLC
Chambersburg PA
CBHW061159180526
45170CB00002B/874